Who Was
Cesar Chavez?

by Dana Meachen Rau

illustrated by Ted Hammond

Penguin Workshop

For teachers everywhere—DMR

For Mom—TH

PENGUIN WORKSHOP
An Imprint of Penguin Random House LLC, New York

Text copyright © 2017 by Dana Meachen Rau.
Illustrations copyright © 2017 by Penguin Random House LLC. All rights reserved.
Published by Penguin Workshop, an imprint of Penguin Random House LLC, New York.
PENGUIN and PENGUIN WORKSHOP are trademarks of Penguin Books Ltd.
WHO HQ & Design is a registered trademark of Penguin Random House LLC.
Manufactured in Guangdong, China.

Visit us online at www.penguinrandomhouse.com.

Library of Congress Control Number: 2017935682

ISBN 9781101995600   10 9 8 7 6 5 4 3 2

Part of the *What Is America?* Boxed Set, ISBN 9780593089781

Who Was Cesar Chavez?

The old theater in Fresno, California, was buzzing with people. A crowd of farmworkers and their families had gathered there for the first meeting of the National Farm Workers Association (NFWA). Cesar Chavez stood on the stage.

He was shy, and not a strong public speaker. But his warm smile and friendly manner drew people in to listen. He had started this union—a group organized to protect workers' rights—to help thousands of farmworkers, including many Mexican Americans, who lived in poverty and were treated unfairly in their jobs.

This day, September 30, 1962, marked the beginning of more than just the farmworkers' union. It was the start of a *movement*—a group of people working together to share an idea and bring about change. Cesar had once worked in the fields himself. He had watched his own family, and many others, suffer to earn enough money to survive. He had a vision for a brighter future for all farmworkers.

Many things were decided at the NFWA's first large meeting. Officers were elected and future plans were discussed. Union members unveiled their flag—a black eagle in a white circle on a red background. The colors had meaning: black for the hard life of the workers, red for the sacrifices they needed to make, and white for hope.

At the meeting, they also agreed on their motto: *Viva La Causa!* (say: VEE-va la COW-sa) Long Live the Cause!

Cesar had worked hard to get the union started, and there was still a long battle ahead. But he was a determined man. He believed in hard work. He believed in sacrificing time and money to help others. He believed in protesting peacefully instead of using violence.

Cesar led a movement that brought major changes to the lives of farmworkers. He also changed the way Mexican Americans were viewed in America. With Cesar's guidance, they came together. They demanded attention. America could no longer ignore them.

CHAPTER 1
The Arizona Ranch

Cesario Estrada Chavez was born on March 31, 1927. His family lived outside the town of Yuma in the Arizona desert. Mama Tella and Papa Chayo, Cesar's grandparents, had come to the United States from Mexico. They had settled near Yuma in the late eighteen hundreds, bought land, and started a ranch.

Papa Chayo died before Cesar was born, but his grandmother still lived in the main adobe house. Cesar, his parents, Librado and Juana, and his brothers and sisters, lived on the ranch, too.

Cesar was the second of six children—older sister, Rita, and younger siblings Richard, Helena,

Vicky, and Lenny. Sadly, Helena died when she was just a baby. At first, the family lived in a room off the main house. They owned only a few pieces of furniture. They had no electricity or running water. When their roof started leaking, the family moved into a cottage on the large ranch.

Cesar and his brother Richard spent their time
exploring, hiking, and playing outdoors together.
They swam in the canal that brought water to the
alfalfa, watermelon, grass, and cotton crops that

grew in the fields. They liked to ride horses and climb trees. The family gathered for barbecues on summer nights with Cesar's aunts, uncles, and many cousins who lived nearby.

But the boys had work to do, too. Cesar's father taught them how to chop wood, work with the horses, weed the crops, and know when the watermelons were ripe. Librado was strict, but patient, as he shared important farming skills with his sons.

Cesar's mother, Juana, wanted her children to grow up to be good people. She taught them to share with others without expecting anything in return. And, even though many Mexican boys were raised to be tough, she did not believe in fighting or violence. Cesar remembered one of her sayings throughout his life: "It takes two to fight, and one can't do it alone." In other words, even if someone wants to fight you, you have the choice to walk away.

The Chavez family was Catholic, but there wasn't a church close by. So Juana and Mama Tella taught the children their religion at home. They gathered around their grandmother's bed at night to hear stories of the saints. The stories of these holy people who had lived very good lives made an impression on young Cesar.

Beginning in 1929, many American banks and businesses went out of business. Millions of people lost their jobs and lived in poverty.

This was known as the Great Depression. During the Depression, it was very difficult to find work. The Chavez family didn't suffer as much as many others, however. Their hard work on the ranch provided them with food—fruit and vegetable crops, fish from the canal, eggs and meat from the chickens, and milk and cheese from the cows. Juana, with her generous heart, even invited less fortunate people over for meals.

When Cesar was six, he was old enough to attend school. But when he arrived at the schoolhouse, the teacher wouldn't let Cesar sit next to his sister, Rita. She asked him to sit with the other children in first grade. He cried and insisted that he have a seat next to Rita. The teacher finally gave in. After a few days, Cesar felt ready to sit with his other first-grade classmates.

But Cesar never really liked school. He would have much rather been outside on the ranch where he wasn't forced to wear shoes! At school, he also discovered how unkind some white people acted toward Mexican Americans.

Cesar's classmates made fun of his brown skin and called him "dirty." They tried to start fights with him. Cesar always spoke Spanish at home with his family. But his teacher hit him on the knuckles with a ruler if she heard him speaking Spanish in the classroom.

At the time, more than 1.5 million Mexicans lived in the United States. Many had come in the early nineteen hundreds, looking for work—and there had been plenty of jobs. But during the Depression, jobs were scarce, and many white people blamed Mexicans. Some were *deported*, or sent back, to Mexico—even if they were American citizens! Those who stayed faced racism in their communities.

Even though the Chavez family was luckier than many during the Depression, by 1933 the ranch itself was in trouble. Arizona suffered from a drought. It had not rained for a long time. The canal was dry and the earth in the fields was cracked. No crops would grow. The family could not pay its bills.

The United States and Mexico

The land that is now California, Nevada, Utah, and parts of Arizona, Colorado, New Mexico, and Wyoming, was once owned by Mexico. In 1848,

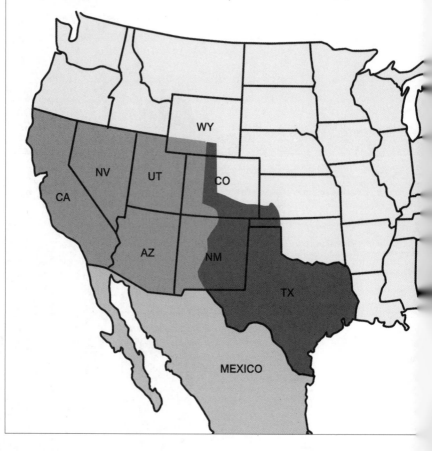

Mexico sold it to the United States for $15 million and the Mexicans living there became American citizens.

During the Mexican Revolution from 1910 to 1920, many more Mexicans fled to the United States hoping for a safer and better life. The United States welcomed these new immigrants because they needed workers for many growing industries—such as agriculture, mining, construction, and transportation.

Even though Mexican Americans worked some of the most difficult jobs, the towns and cities where they lived were segregated for many years. There were stores, restaurants, and schools for Mexicans and separate businesses and schools for white people.

Mexican territory annexed in 1845

Territories lost by Mexico in 1848–1853

Hundreds of thousands of other Americans who had lost their jobs headed to California to find work. California was suffering from the Great Depression, too.

But there was no drought in California. And because the state has some of the richest farmland in the world, workers were needed to pick crops, which included tomatoes, lettuce, grapes, avocados, strawberries, peas, cherries, and corn. So in 1938, Cesar's father headed west to California. He hoped to earn enough money to support his family and save the ranch.

CHAPTER 2
Hard Work for Little Pay

Cesar's father, Librado, found work in the bean fields of Oxnard, California. Soon after, he sent for his family to come and join him. They moved into a tiny house with a worn fence in a crowded Mexican neighborhood called a *barrio* (say: BA-ree-o). The children went to school for only half the day, and helped their parents in the

afternoons. Cesar missed the wide-open spaces of his home in the Arizona desert. "I was like a wild duck with its wings clipped," he said. "I felt trapped." After a little over a month, they returned to Yuma. Librado tried hard to keep the ranch, but he couldn't afford it. So the Chavez family moved to California for good in June 1939. Cesar was twelve years old.

In California, most farms were owned by wealthy landowners who sold their crops to large corporations. They employed thousands of people to work in their fields. These workers were called *migrants* because they *migrated*— or moved—from town to town in Southern and Central California according to the seasons of crops. Summer was busiest, when they picked lima beans, avocados, corn, chilies, grapes, and tomatoes. They picked cotton throughout the fall until the end of the year. In winter and early spring, they picked carrots, cauliflower, broccoli, and cabbage. Spring was the time for melons, beans, and cherries.

The migrant laborers worked hard. But employers did not treat them fairly. They paid them late, and sometimes not at all. To earn enough money for the family, Librado, Juana, Cesar, and most of his brothers and sisters worked, too. But on some days, the whole Chavez family combined earned only thirty cents! The bosses would miscount their sacks of potatoes or make up a lower number for the cotton scale on purpose. Sometimes they refused to pay them what they had promised.

Farm work was difficult and unhealthy. The growers did not provide water for their laborers— even in the summer heat. The fields did not have bathrooms nearby, so workers had to use the fields they worked in. In the winter, the ground was cold and slippery with mud. Short-handled hoes, called *cortitos* (say: kor-TEE-toes), were brutal on workers' backs when they leaned over to use them.

Even breathing was dangerous. Farmworkers often inhaled *pesticides*—the poisonous chemicals sprayed on the crops to kill bugs.

This was not the life that families had imagined for themselves when they arrived in California. They had hoped to find respect, work, and the possibility of a better future. The money they earned was barely enough to pay for food, gas, or rent. They were constantly on the move to new fields to find ripe crops to pick, just to earn enough money to survive.

The California farm owners didn't see any reason to treat their employees well. If anyone complained, they could simply hire another worker to take his or her place. Not just Mexicans, but Filipino and other Asian immigrants, African

Americans, and poor whites made up the three hundred thousand Americans who had resettled in California to work in the fields. Many didn't speak English. And many didn't know how to read because they didn't have the time to go to school. The wealthy, mostly white, growers held all the power and could easily take advantage of them.

Some farms and orchards provided camps for workers to live in. But these camps were crowded and dirty, packed with hundreds of people sleeping in tents. Often, only one faucet provided water for fifty or more families. Sickness spread easily.

Juana didn't want her family in the camps. Instead, they looked for other places to live: in barns, shacks, garages, and even their car. They spent one Oxnard winter living in a tent that puddled with rain. They couldn't always afford to buy food, so they collected wild mustard greens near the canals where they caught muddy fish to eat.

Even when the Chavez family was in a town for only a few days, Juana insisted her children go to school. Other kids teased Cesar for being so poor and for wearing the same shirt every day. They made fun of his Mexican accent. If they challenged him to fights, Cesar kept his mother's lessons in mind and walked away. But he spent his days at school frightened of his teacher and the other students.

Racism against Mexican Americans didn't happen only at school. Now that Cesar was moving from town to town, he saw segregation in many communities. Signs in shop windows read "Whites only. No Mexicans." Public swimming

pools only let nonwhites swim on certain days of the week. Theaters reserved the middle, best seats for white people.

By the time Cesar finished eighth grade, he had attended more than thirty different schools! He refused to continue on to high school. His family needed him, and so Cesar began working in the fields full-time when he was only fifteen years old.

CHAPTER 3
Growing as a Leader

In 1943, when Cesar was sixteen, he walked into a shop in Delano. There he saw a girl with flowers in her hair, eating a snow cone with friends. Her name was Helen Fabela. Unlike Cesar, she attended high school. But she also worked in the California fields with her parents when she had days off. Cesar and Helen began dating.

But then Cesar decided that he needed a break from the fields.

Helen Fabela

He joined the navy and left California. World War II was over, but the navy seemed like a good opportunity for Cesar. He traveled to Saipan and Guam, two islands in the western Pacific Ocean. He worked as a low-ranking seaman. But Cesar didn't like navy life. He didn't like being ordered around.

After two years, Cesar returned to California. In 1948, he and Helen got married. Cesar worked at a variety of jobs while his family grew. He and Helen had three children by the time Cesar was twenty-three years old. He found a job sorting and stacking wood at a lumberyard in the town of San Jose. They moved into a poor barrio on the east side of town called Sal Si Puedes (say: sal see PWAY-dess), which, in English, means "escape if you can."

In east San Jose, Cesar met Father Donald McDonnell. McDonnell was a Catholic priest who talked with Cesar about the need for all people, including farmworkers, to be treated fairly and with respect. Father McDonnell shared many of his books with Cesar. He was especially interested in Gandhi, a political leader in India who believed in peace and nonviolence.

Mahatma (Mohandas) Gandhi (1869–1948)

Born and raised in Western India, Mohandas Gandhi attended law school in London. He became interested in the struggle for civil rights while working as a lawyer in South Africa.

Once back in India, Gandhi worked hard to free his homeland from British rule. He was called "Mahatma"—a term that means both wise and holy. But he did not fight with weapons. He believed in showing love and kindness to others. He broke laws he didn't agree with, but he always faced his enemies peacefully. Gandhi proved that peaceful resistance can be a powerful force for change.

Gandhi is known as the "father of the nation" in India.

In 1952, a man named Fred Ross arrived in Sal Si Puedes. Fred and others had founded a group called the Community Service Organization (CSO) in Los Angeles to battle the racism against Mexican Americans from police, schools, employers, and the government. He wanted to expand the CSO

Fred Ross

in Mexican American communities all over California. Cesar didn't trust Fred at first. After all, Fred was a white man. How would he know about the problems of Mexican Americans? But Cesar realized that Fred truly believed in fairness and helping others. And Fred was impressed with Cesar. He was looking for volunteers to work for the CSO. And Cesar was eager to help.

Fred gave Cesar his first task—to knock on doors in the barrio and ask people to register to vote. The CSO believed that if more Mexican Americans voted in elections for the leaders *they* wanted, then their *civil rights*—their basic rights as American citizens—would be protected.

Fred had estimated that California held one-quarter of all Mexicans living in the United States. Not all of the Mexicans in the barrios were US citizens. So, in addition to registering people, Cesar also helped set up citizenship classes for them.

Cesar was nervous knocking on strangers' doors. He was a small, soft-spoken man. But soon his confidence grew. The more he spoke with people, the more sure he became about the important work of the CSO.

Cesar was very busy. By 1952, he and Helen had four children, all age three and under. He volunteered for the CSO in an office in San Jose that also served as a community center for Mexican Americans. Cesar would get frustrated by all the stories he heard from the people at the community center. Some had been beaten by the police, or were in danger of being deported. He would assist them as best he could.

Cesar was only in his midtwenties, but he was already becoming a strong leader for Mexican Americans and farmworkers. He became a full-time paid employee of the CSO. Now Cesar's job went beyond his own community into towns and cities all around California. He would hold small meetings at first, to meet with Mexican Americans in their own homes. The meetings became much larger as support and interest grew. Cesar found plenty of volunteers to help. Once a CSO chapter was up and running, he moved on to another town.

In 1958, Cesar discovered that one of the main problems facing the Mexican American farmworkers was the *bracero* (say: bra-SARE-o) program. Growers brought in temporary workers from Mexico to work the jobs that legally belonged to American citizens (mostly Mexican Americans) who lived in California.

Cesar asked for a government investigation. He was determined to prove that growers were breaking the law.

Cesar's bosses at the CSO recognized what a strong leader Cesar had become. He had helped register tens of thousands of new voters. He had helped unite the Mexican American community.

So in 1959, the CSO named Cesar its national director. He, Helen, and their now eight children moved to Los Angeles. Cesar would be in charge of running Community Service Organizations all over California and Arizona.

Braceros

During World War II (1939–1945), the US government made a law that allowed farm owners to bring in temporary workers from Mexico when their crops were ready to be picked. The jobs were available because many of the local employees had left to fight the war. The Mexican people who came to the United States to fill these jobs were called *braceros.*

After the war was over, many growers still used braceros. They paid them very little and housed them in dirty, crowded, and dangerous camps. Braceros had no protection under the law because they were not citizens. They could be sent back to Mexico at any time.

The bracero system helped only the landowners. It was unfair to both the US farmworkers and the braceros.

CHAPTER 4
The NFWA

In the early 1960s, migrant workers constantly struggled to find work. Many made only about $1,000 a year, which was impossible to live on. The work they did was often dangerous. Landowners and farm bosses treated them with very little respect as human beings.

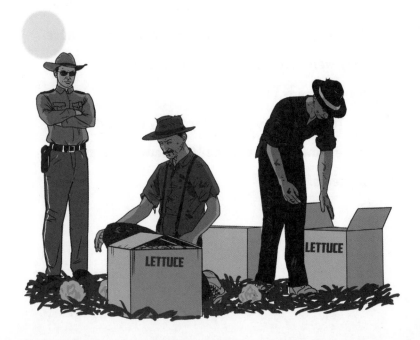

Cesar wanted to organize farmworkers into a *union*—a group of employees organized to *negotiate* (to sit down and discuss) with employers about the terrible working conditions of the migrants. There were many unions in place by the 1960s, including those for warehouse workers, teachers, firefighters, miners, truck drivers, and other industries. Cesar felt a farmworkers union would be able to negotiate better pay and safer working conditions with the growers.

In 1962, after only a few years as director, Cesar resigned from the CSO. He wanted to start a farmworkers union on his own terms. Cesar and his family moved back to Delano. Many of Helen and Cesar's relatives still lived there and could help support them. Cesar and Helen had very little money saved. So Helen picked crops in the fields and Cesar took on odd jobs, either in the fields or building houses for his brother Richard, who was a carpenter.

Cesar spent most of his time driving from town to town in the valley around Delano, the San Joaquin Valley, to talk to migrant workers. He held meetings in their homes and listened to their problems.

Cesar planned to build the union one farmworker at a time. But many didn't believe growers would ever listen to their concerns. They were scared to join a union.

The farmworkers were nervous because their employers had a lot of power and money.

When they had stood up to their bosses in the past, they had been beaten, fired, thrown in jail, or deported. So Cesar tried to keep the meetings secret. He didn't want the growers to punish workers for simply talking about forming a union.

Cesar even tried not to call his organization a union. He called it a *movement* and hoped that it would bring a big change in the way poor, hardworking people were treated. But Cesar couldn't do such a big job on his own. He worked closely with Dolores Huerta, a woman he had met through the CSO.

While Cesar was quiet and friendly, Dolores was more outspoken. They made a good pair. Cesar's cousin Manuel and his brother Richard also helped Cesar to print flyers about the union and passed them out with the help of their children, nieces, and nephews. Through it all, he still got advice from Fred Ross. Cesar surrounded himself with people he trusted and who were willing to give up their time and money. He worked with people who believed that change was needed in America's treatment of farmworkers.

Dolores Huerta (1930–)

Dolores Clara Fernandez Huerta was raised in Stockton, California. Even as a young girl, she was interested in the rights of all people to be treated fairly and equally. Dolores led the Stockton chapter of the Community Service Organization in 1955. And in 1962, she cofounded the National Farm Workers Association with Cesar Chavez.

In 2012, Dolores was awarded the Presidential Medal of Freedom by President Barack Obama. She continues to speak out for the rights of workers, women, and children.

They decided to call their union the National Farm Workers Association (NFWA). As members joined, they paid monthly dues that kept the union going. Cesar spent a lot of time in his home office making calls and writing letters. Dolores and Manuel took to the fields to talk to farmworkers. Helen Chavez was in charge of keeping track of costs. At times, uniting so many people seemed like an impossible task.

But Cesar had faith that it could happen. "The desire to win has got to be very strong," he said, "or else you can't do it."

After about six months, the NFWA had enough members to hold one large meeting. About one hundred fifty members and their families met on September 30, 1962, in the town of Fresno.

Together they decided that their first goal would be to try to get the governor of California to set a minimum wage for workers. A *minimum wage* is a price paid per hour of work that landowners could not go below. And the NFWA wanted to have a say in what that wage would be. At the meeting, they unveiled their new flag with the strong symbol of an eagle. Everyone shouted the NFWA motto: *Viva La Causa!* Long Live the Cause!

As the union grew, Richard fixed up an old church in Delano as the new NFWA office. The union started a newspaper, called *El Malcriado* (say: el mal-kree-AH-doe). The name meant "those who talk back" and sometimes refers to children with bad manners. The NFWA was ready to "talk back" to their employers about how unfairly they were treated in the fields. Since many farmworkers couldn't read, cartoons played a big part in communicating the NFWA's message: growers were abusing the workers and the union could help them. They sold their paper

at barrio grocery stores for ten cents.

A strike was one of the best tools unions could use against unfair employers. During a strike, workers would refuse to pick crops. They wanted to pressure their bosses into negotiating with them. They would march with signs, called *picketing*, to make their demands known. Cesar had wanted the union to have more members before asking anyone to stop working and launching a major strike. But he couldn't hold off striking much longer.

Another union, made up mostly of Filipino workers, was planning a strike against grape growers in Delano who refused to pay them the

Larry Itliong

same salary that they had received from other growers. Larry Itliong was the leader of the Agricultural Workers Organizing Committee (AWOC) in Delano. He asked the NFWA to join them in the strike. If the two unions worked together, they could make a bigger difference.

At first, Cesar wasn't sure his group was ready. They had only a little over one thousand members. But he realized that a strike was the only way to get the growers to listen. And, if he did his best to spread news of the strike beyond Delano, he might be able to draw attention to the issues facing farmworkers. So the NFWA joined the AWOC in their strike against the Delano grape growers.

CHAPTER 5
Refusing to Be Ignored

Starting on September 20, 1965, NFWA union members did not go to work. Instead, they joined the AWOC members and picketed on the roads along the many acres of grape fields, called *vineyards*. They carried signs that read

"Huelga!" (say: WEL-ga) which means *strike* in Spanish. They chanted *"Huelga! Huelga! Huelga!"* And they shouted to the workers still in the fields to join them.

Days and weeks went by. The growers became very upset that they had lost so many workers. They were surprised that a poor Mexican American like Cesar was brave and smart enough to make such an impact. They played loud music to drown out the shouts of the strikers. They turned their dogs on them, sprayed them with

pesticides, and even threatened them with guns.

The police did nothing to help. Instead, they harassed the strikers, too. In October, the county sheriff even made it illegal to use the word *huelga.* He said the noise disturbed the workers still in the fields. A group of strikers, including Helen, still shouted *"Huelga!"* They were arrested and spent a few days in jail. Through it all, Cesar insisted that the strikers remain peaceful and not fight back. "Violence can only hurt us and our cause," he said.

As Cesar hoped, the strike drew attention from people outside of the Delano area. Reporters came from other US cities to write stories about what was happening there. Cesar spoke at colleges to get volunteers to support their strike.

Soon students, church leaders, lawyers, government officials, and national labor organizations offered to help them. Cesar was pleased. "It's amazing they all work together. That's the miracle of it all," he said. Volunteers gave time, money, and donations of food and clothing. Some even marched with them on picket lines.

It was very difficult for the workers to stay on strike. They weren't earning any money and couldn't pay their bills. Some left the area to find jobs elsewhere. Some picked different crops for other growers. Some even went back to work for the grape growers. But the migrants who did stay with the strike believed their goal was worth fighting for.

To make sure their grapes didn't rot on the vines, the growers brought in pickers from outside the San Joaquin Valley. They came from Mexico and from poor neighborhoods in the city of Los Angeles. Then winter arrived and the growers didn't even need workers. The strike seemed to be losing its energy.

So Cesar decided to affect the growers in a different way. He sent out volunteers to block the grape deliveries on loading docks in Los Angeles and San Francisco. He didn't want any of the grapes that had been picked to arrive at grocery stores and markets. He also urged people to *boycott*—to refuse to buy—grapes from companies that were unfair to their workers.

News of the situation in Delano had reached the US government in Washington, DC. Some members of Congress were working toward changing the National Labor Relations Act to finally protect farmworkers. The National Labor Relations Act had been passed in 1935 to give employees in many industries the right to form labor unions that would help protect their rights to fair wages and safe workplaces. But it specifically did *not* include farmworkers.

On March 14, 1966, Senator Robert F. Kennedy and other members of Congress came to Delano to discuss the issue. The committee questioned the sheriff, who had arrested strikers who hadn't broken any laws. Senator Kennedy scolded him and told him to take some time during his lunch break to read the Constitution of the United States!

The strike had been going on for about six months. Workers wouldn't be needed in the vineyards for months, so Cesar wanted to find a way to keep everyone's attention. He wanted to remind the entire country that the strike was still going on in Delano. He decided to lead a march to Sacramento, the capital of California.

Cesar believed that people marching together would draw more attention to the strike. It would unite the farmworkers. And it would help grow the union by bringing in even more members as they passed through barrios along the route from Delano to Sacramento. He hoped that when he arrived at the capitol, Governor Pat Brown would be willing to talk to him about the importance of making grape growers recognize their workers' unions.

About seventy people, including members of the NFWA and the AWOC, started out on March 17, 1966. But they faced trouble before they even left Delano. The chief of police, and about thirty officers, locked arms and blocked the street. Cesar said to them, "We'll stay here if it takes a year." The police finally gave in and let the marchers pass.

The three-hundred-mile walk from Delano to Sacramento would take twenty-five days. Early on, Cesar's leg started to swell. His back was in pain. He had a fever. But he walked on.

As the marchers continued on their journey to the capital, workers left the fields to join them. People in towns greeted them with cheers, music, food to eat, and places to sleep. Reporters followed along, and the story appeared in newspapers across the country.

When they were about a week away from Sacramento, one of Cesar's volunteers brought him some news. Schenley Industries, one of the major grape growers, wanted to meet with him! The strike and boycott were hurting Schenley's business. The company was willing to sign a contract to recognize the unions! The growers were willing to negotiate better wages and conditions for workers.

The marchers reached Sacramento on Easter Sunday, April 10. A crowd of more than eight thousand supporters gathered in the park across from the capitol building. The governor was away on vacation. When he offered to meet with Cesar the very next day, Cesar refused. He wanted to show the governor that he was sick of his excuses.

Cesar, Dolores, and others spoke to the crowd about their hopes for the future of the movement.

In August 1966, the NFWA became even stronger when Larry Itliong and Cesar combined their two unions into one and called it the United Farm Workers Organizing Committee (UFWOC). Later that year, to show support for the union's successes, the Reverend Martin Luther King Jr. sent Cesar a telegram that read: "Our separate struggles are really one—a struggle for freedom, for dignity, and for humanity."

Telegram **WESTERN UNION** Telegram

Mr. Cesar Chaves
United Farm Work Organising Committee
P.O Box 130
Delano, California

Martin Luther King Jr. (1929–1968)

Martin Luther King was an American Baptist minister and leader of the African American civil rights movement. He led many peaceful marches and protests to highlight the unfair treatment of black people in the South. In 1963, he helped organize the March on Washington, where he gave his famous "I Have a Dream" speech. In 1964, he received the Nobel Peace Prize. He was assassinated on April 4, 1968, in Memphis, Tennessee.

By the summer of 1967, the grape strike was finishing its second year. The union had signed contracts with some of the grape growers in Delano, but there were still hundreds of thousands of farmworkers who were not protected. As always, Cesar was determined to do more.

CHAPTER 6
Ending the Great Grape Strike

Cesar had always believed that peaceful actions were more powerful than violence. But not all union members agreed with him. They were frustrated that the strike was still going on. And while the union did its best to take care of their needs, they were still living in poverty. Some union members destroyed the growers' property or threatened workers in the fields to get their bosses' attention.

Cesar knew these violent actions would hurt the way people saw the union. He thought of Gandhi and the tools he had used to help bring change to India. Gandhi had often fasted— stopped eating for a period of time—to make a point. So Cesar decided to do the same.

He stopped eating on February 15, 1968, and he planned to fast until the UFWOC members agreed to stop using violence against the growers. His sacrifice of food was meant to remind union members of the sacrifices of time, money, and energy they still needed to make to keep the union going and to keep their community strong.

During the fast, Cesar stayed at the new union headquarters—called the Forty Acres—on the edge of Delano. Thousands of people came to visit him. They treated the Forty Acres like a holy place.

Forty Acres

They lit candles, hung religious symbols, and held church services. Some women even painted the windows of Cesar's room to look like the stained glass windows of a church. During the day, Cesar stayed in bed, reading, sleeping, or trying to do work.

In the evenings, he met with visitors. People waited in two-hour lines just to talk to him. Donations poured in as word spread about Cesar's fast.

But not eating was hard on Cesar. He had horrible pains in his head, stomach, legs, and back. He lost more than thirty pounds. Helen told him he was crazy. She was worried for his health.

The doctors were worried, too. Even Senator Kennedy urged him to stop his fast. Finally, Cesar decided he had made his point. He ended his fast after twenty-five days at a ceremony at Delano Park on March 10, 1968.

Helen and Cesar Chavez with Senator Kennedy (center)

Thousands of people, including the senator, gathered to share in the event.

Only a few days after Cesar's fast ended, Senator Kennedy announced that he was running for president. Cesar and Dolores Huerta quickly agreed to support him. They campaigned for the senator all over California.

On June 5, 1968, they were both with Kennedy in Los Angeles. Dolores even stood next to him as he gave a speech. But as Kennedy left the event, he was shot and killed. It was a national tragedy. Many were sure he would go on to win the Democratic nomination, and maybe the presidency.

Robert F. Kennedy wasn't the first civil rights supporter to be killed that year. Martin Luther King Jr. had been assassinated just two months earlier. By this time, Cesar Chavez had become a national celebrity. His supporters worried that his life might be in danger, too. But instead of hiding, Cesar used his celebrity status to force all the growers to pay attention.

He called for an even larger boycott. He sent out UFWOC volunteers to spread the message to major cities in the United States and even into Canada. Cesar asked people to stop buying *all* the grapes grown in the state of California. He reminded them that the grapes on their table came with a price—the hard work of the poor farmworkers who suffered in the fields.

Union volunteers met with mayors of major cities. Volunteers built up groups of supporters wherever they went, including students, businesspeople, religious people, politicians, and homemakers. They picketed grocery stores and told people not only to boycott grapes, but to boycott the stores that sold them!

By 1970, the growers had lost millions of dollars from the boycott. Many had to sell off their farmland. The Delano growers couldn't fight against the strength of the union and the national attention any longer. So they met with Cesar. They discussed the workers' demands. And a large group of growers finally agreed to sign contracts with the UFWOC.

On July 29, 1970, the grape growers came to the Forty Acres. Cesar sat with them in front of a large crowd. They were all in a cheerful mood—the strike and boycott were finally over. The union signed contracts with twenty-nine growers that day. The Great Delano Grape Strike, as it had become known, had lasted five years. Cesar had never planned to give up. "We were going to stay with the struggle if it took a lifetime," he said. "And we meant it."

The strike had been about more than grapes.

It had shown the country how the poor and powerless deserved the rights promised to all Americans. The strikers had sacrificed a lot. But they had gained a lot, too. The contracts promised a wage of $1.80 an hour, a health plan, protection against pesticides, and more. Cesar's movement had brought positive changes to thousands of farmworkers' lives.

Now that the battle over grapes was finished, the union could devote more time to farmworkers who were picking other crops and who had also been looking to the UFWOC for help. Cesar turned his attention to the lettuce fields of the Salinas Valley.

After the lettuce growers saw what had happened at Delano, they decided to let their workers unionize. But instead of signing with the UFWOC, lettuce pickers signed contracts with another union called the Teamsters. The Teamsters had been around since 1903.

Their union was originally formed by wagon and truck drivers. But they were known for being dishonest in the way they ran their union. Some people said that they cared more about the bosses and managers than the workers. They were often accused of violence and bullying.

So Cesar called for a lettuce strike and boycott. In December 1970, Cesar was arrested for ignoring a law against the boycott and was sent to jail.

In his cell, Cesar spent his days reading, answering letters, and meeting with visitors, including Robert F. Kennedy's widow, Ethel, and Martin Luther King Jr.'s widow, Coretta. Outside, crowds held vigils and rallies to support him. Cesar was released just before Christmas. "They can jail us," he said, "but they can never jail the Cause."

Cesar Chavez and Coretta Scott King lead a lettuce boycott march in New York City.

CHAPTER 7
Protests and Peace

In the 1970s, Cesar moved the union's headquarters to a quiet, remote, 187-acre California community called La Paz. Cesar had always wanted a place for union members to live together in a peaceful setting. Here, people shared dormitories, community gardens, kitchens, a church, and an educational center. The wide-open space reminded Cesar of his childhood on the ranch. Also around this time, the union was renamed the United Farm Workers of America (UFW).

But not everything about the union was peaceful. Cesar didn't always listen to other people's ideas. If they disagreed with him, he would fire them. The union fought growers in courts not only in California, but also in Arizona, Kansas, Idaho, Oregon, Florida, and other states where farmworkers were employed. When union contracts with growers expired, many farmworkers signed on with the Teamsters union instead of the UFW. Times were tough, but Dolores Huerta came up with a new slogan to keep them going: *¡Sí, se puede!* (say: see say PWAY-day). Yes, it can be done!

¡Sí Se Puede!

Luckily, there was a new governor in California, Jerry Brown. Governor Brown was very interested in the rights of farmworkers. It seemed Cesar might finally have the government support he needed! National labor laws in

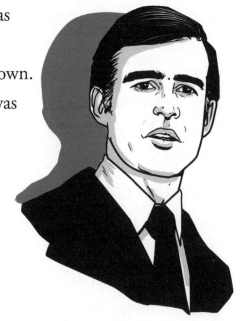

Jerry Brown

the United States still didn't protect the rights of farmworkers to join the unions of their choice. Governor Brown was willing to do something about it. He gathered the UFW, the Teamsters, and the growers in separate rooms. He went from room to room and helped them agree on a deal. Governor Brown signed the Agricultural Labor Relations Act into law on June 5, 1975.

Finally, a law protected the rights of workers to choose the union they wanted.

By the 1980s, Cesar had done more than just build a union for farmworkers. He had shown the world that poor people who were victims of racism and unfair laws could come together, organize themselves, and make changes in their lives. Their rewards were higher wages, vacation time, medical plans, portable toilets, and access to fresh drinking water in the fields. They could finally save money and buy their own homes. Their children could finish high school instead of having to work in the fields as Cesar had done.

Mexican Americans were even getting more involved in politics to help make the laws that affected their lives.

In a 1984 speech, Cesar said, "We have looked into the future and the future is ours." He was referring not only to Mexican Americans, but to Latinos—those from Spanish-speaking countries and territories, such as Cuba, Puerto Rico, and the Dominican Republic—all over the United States.

Cesar continued to work on other issues, including the use of pesticides in the fields.

He fasted again, starting in July 1988, to draw attention to the cause. He was more than sixty years old, and he grew very weak over the thirty-six days of not eating.

Growers continued to use pesticides. But Cesar continued to give speeches all over the United States about the problems facing farmworkers and the future of the Latino community. When he wasn't traveling, he spent time with his family—his eight children and many grandchildren.

In April 1993, Cesar was called to defend the union at a trial. He went to San Luis, Arizona, near where he had grown up. He was staying with some friends. After a long day of questioning at the courthouse, he went to bed. When his friends checked on him in the morning, they discovered that he had died in his sleep.

His body had been weak since his last fast. He was only sixty-six years old.

A few days later, on April 29, 1993, a funeral was held in Delano. Tens of thousands of people came. A three-mile-long procession walked the streets, carrying flowers and flags. Cesar's brother Richard built him a pine coffin. His body was buried at La Paz.

Since his death, Cesar has received many honors, including the Aguila Azteca, the highest award given to foreign citizens by the Mexican government, and the Presidential Medal of Freedom by President Clinton. Parks, schools, libraries, streets, and community centers have been named for him across America.

In 2012, President Barack Obama made La Paz, the union's headquarters, a national monument. The president also declared March 31, Cesar's birthday, as Cesar Chavez Day. He called upon all Americans to celebrate the achievements of Cesar across the United States by helping out in their communities.

"Yes, We Can!"

In 2008, Barack Obama, inspired by the slogan "¡Sí, Se Puede!" used a similar motto, "Yes, We Can," for his presidential campaign.

Cesar Chavez has become a symbol of hope for the poor and powerless. He remains an inspiration to Latinos everywhere, and a strong but peaceful hero in the fight against racism in America. Cesar proved that people who come together and speak with one voice can be much stronger than one person standing alone.

Timeline of Cesar Chavez's Life

1927	Cesario Estrada Chavez born on March 31 near Yuma, Arizona
1939	Cesar's family leaves their Arizona ranch behind and moves to California where they work as migrant farmworkers
1946	Joins the navy and serves for two years
1948	Marries Helen Fabela on October 22; the couple eventually has eight children
1952	Meets Fred Ross and starts working with him for the Community Service Organization (CSO)
1959	Named national director of the CSO
1962	Leaves the CSO to start the National Farm Workers Association (NFWA)
1965	Agrees to join the strike against grape growers in the San Joaquin Valley
1966	Leads a 300-mile march from Delano to California's capitol building in Sacramento in March and April
1968	Calls for a boycott of grapes grown in California
1970	Grape growers sign contracts on July 29, ending the five-year grape strike
1975	The Agricultural Labor Relations Act is passed on June 5
1988	Cesar fasts for thirty-six days to bring attention to the pesticide issue
1993	Dies in San Luis, Arizona, on April 23

Timeline of the World

1910–1920	Mexican citizens rise up against an unfair government during the Mexican Revolution
1920	The Nineteenth Amendment to the US Constitution grants women the right to vote
1929–1939	The Great Depression hits the United States, resulting in unemployment and homelessness
1952	The de Havilland Comet 1, the first large commercial jet airliner, starts flying passengers
1953	Sir Edmund Hillary and Tenzing Norgay climb to the summit of Mount Everest, the highest mountain in the world
1959	Hawaii officially becomes the fiftieth state on August 21
1964	The Beatles appear on *The Ed Sullivan Show* on February 9 and start the British Invasion of American music charts
1976	Steve Jobs and Steve Wozniak start Apple Computer Inc., which has since become a major world leader in personal computers and technology
1977	The first Star Wars movie is released and becomes a worldwide hit
1980	Mount Saint Helens, a volcano in Washington State, erupts, sending ash and gas fifteen miles high
1989	The Berlin Wall, separating the city of Berlin, Germany, comes down
1990	The Hubble Space Telescope is launched into orbit
1993	Beanie Babies are first sold by Ty Warner USA

Bibliography

* Books for young readers

*Brimner, Larry Dane. *Strike! The Farm Workers' Fight for their Rights*. Honesdale, PA: Calkins Creek, 2014.

Cesar Chavez. Directed by Diego Luna. Santa Monica, CA: Lionsgate, 2014.

Ferriss, Susan, and Ricardo Sandoval. *The Fight in the Fields: Cesar Chavez and the Farmworkers Movement*. New York: Harcourt, Brace and Company, 1997.

"Latino Americans." PBS. pbs.org/latino-americans/en/watch-videos/#2365075996.

Levy, Jacques E. *Cesar Chavez: Autobiography of La Causa*. New York: W.W. Norton & Company Inc., 1975.

Lindsey, Robert. "Cesar Chavez, 66, Organizer of Union For Migrants, Dies." *New York Times*. April 24, 1993. http://www.nytimes.com/1993/04/24/obituaries/cesar-chavez-66-organizer-of-union-for-migrants-dies.html (accessed September 2015).

Pawel, Miriam. *The Crusades of Cesar Chavez*. New York: Bloomsbury Press, 2014.

Websites

www.chavezfoundation.org

www.ufw.org